WASEEM CHAUHAN

Meet Waseem, a Computer Science gradated Educational Leader. After realising that pr eating Doritos and drinking Irn-Bru might initially seemed, Waseem decided to try his ha

For several years, Waseem travelled the world, sharing his knowledge and love of all things tech with students of all ages. He eventually settled down in the Midlands, where he started a family and continued to teach while also taking on leadership roles. As an Assistant Headteacher, Waseem worked tirelessly to improve the learning experience for his students, primarily through a series of motivational phrases such as *'the bell doesn't dismiss you, I dismiss you'* and *'if you waste my time now, I'll waste your time... after school'*.

Recently, Waseem decided to switch things up and try something new. He left the classroom and became a Delivery Manager, using his strong organisational and leadership skills to guide teams and bring projects to completion. Despite moving on from teaching, Waseem's love of education and desire to make a positive impact on the world remain as strong as ever. Plus, now he gets to wear business casual instead of a shirt and tie every day, which is a major win in his book.

Beyond their career in delivery, Waseem is a published author with a Udemy course on Agile and a collection of children's books. A lifelong enthusiast of philosophy, they have long explored its relevance to modern life and decision-making. This book marks their first foray into writing on the subject, blending deep philosophical inquiry with practical insights.

For more insights, visit Waseem.ch

ALSO BY WASEEM CHAUHAN

The Ultimate Guide to Understanding Agile & Passing the PSM1 Certification: Mastering Agile
The Internet Adventures of Michael, Dua & Zane

WASEEM CHAUHAN

Harmonies of Thought

How 80s Pop Explores Life's Big Questions

Copyright © 2025 Waseem Chauhan
ISBN: 9798314573693

All rights reserved. No part of this book may be reproduced, distributed, or transmitted in any form or by any means, including photocopying, recording, or other electronic or mechanical methods, without the prior written permission of the author, except in the case of brief quotations used in reviews or critical articles.

For permission requests, please contact the author at Waseem.ch

To my amazing wife, Rubina, for being my constant support.

To my kids, for providing just the right amount of noise to keep me grounded (and never too focused).

And to all those who patiently listened to my endless musings on 80s pop and philosophy, thank you!

Contents

INTRODUCTION

ONE   The Human League - Don't You Want Me

TWO   Kenny Loggins - Footloose

THREE   Huey Lewis and the News - The Power of Love

FOUR   Madonna - Material Girl

FIVE   Eurythmics - Sweet Dreams

SIX   Foreigner - I Want to Know What Love Is

SEVEN   Journey - Don't Stop Believin'

EIGHT   The Police - Every Little Thing She Does Is Magic

NINE   Bonnie Tyler - Total Eclipse of the Heart

TEN   Rick Springfield - Jessie's Girl

ELEVEN   Culture Club - Karma Chameleon

TWELVE   Whitney Houston - I Want to Dance with Somebody

THIRTEEN   Survivor - Eye of the Tiger

FOURTEEN   Van Halen - Jump

FIFTEEN   Guns N' Rose - Sweet Child o' Mine

CLOSING THOUGHTS

INTRODUCTION

Amongst all types of human expression, music and philosophy stand as pillars of insight, each offering a unique lens through which to understand the complexities of existence. In Harmonies of Thought I show how these two profound forms of human creativity are a reflection of one another, inviting you on a journey through the lyrical landscapes of music, accompanied by the guiding wisdom of philosophical thought.

I will lead you through a lyrical odyssey with the resonance of existential inquiry. Each set of lyrics is a gateway to philosophical reflection, and I invite you to reflect on how your favourite songs are echoes of the great philosophies of all time. Enjoy the illumination of the intersections between music and philosophy, revealing the rich tapestry of insight that emerges when these two realms converge.

As we journey through these pages, you will understand that these melodies not only rock us on the dance floor but echo the wisdom that reverberate through the history of philosophical thought. In the harmonies of music and the depths of philosophy, we discover the essence of human experience and philosophy.

So, tune your ears to the melodies of the soul, and open your mind to the wisdom of the ages. You are about to experience the melodies of human experience, revealing the timeless truths that bind us all together in the grand symphony of existence.

The Human League

Don't You Want Me

*You were working as a waitress in a cocktail bar
When I met you
I picked you out, I shook you up
And turned you around
Turned you into someone new
Now five years later on you've got the world at your feet
Success has been so easy for you
But don't forget it's me who put you where
And I can put you back down too.*

This song is an assertion of power and control over another person's life. Friedrich Nietzsche's concept of the *will-to-power* which explores the dynamics of power is very relevant here. This concept is central to his philosophy, particularly explored in his later works, such as *Beyond Good and Evil* and *Thus Spoke Zarathustra* which all point towards his thinking that individuals and societies are driven by a desire for power and dominance.

The Will to Power
According to Nietzsche, the *will-to-power* is not merely an instinct for survival or a drive for pleasure, it is the essential force that drives all life. Essentially, the *will-to-power* subsumes and reinterprets other motivations such as pleasure seeking, moral duty, or happiness, seeing them as manifestations of a deeper, more primal drive that is not limited to rational thought. Nietzsche argued that these explanations are superficial and fail to capture the depth of human experience. For Nietzsche, pleasure and pain are secondary to the more fundamental drive of the *will-to-power*. People endure suffering and hardship not

just to avoid pain or to seek pleasure, but to overcome challenges and to achieve a sense of power and mastery.

Nietzsche states that the *will-to-power* is the core driving force of all living beings. The *will-to-power* involves an intrinsic desire to assert and enhance one's own power and influence. It is an ongoing process of self-overcoming, where individuals constantly strive to grow, improve, and assert their dominance or influence over their environment and themselves.

The will to power offers explanations for all aspects of human behaviour:
Ambition and Achievement: Human ambition, the desire to achieve and excel, can be seen as manifestations of the *will-to-power*. People strive to reach higher positions in their careers, gain recognition, and achieve their goals as expressions of this fundamental drive.

Creativity and Art: Artistic and creative endeavours can also be understood through the lens of the *will-to-power*. Artists and creators push the boundaries of what is known and express themselves in ways that transcend ordinary experiences, thereby exercising their *will-to-power*.

Social Dynamics: Interpersonal relationships and social structures are also influenced by the *will-to-power*. Hierarchies, power struggles, and social movements can all be interpreted as expressions of this underlying drive for influence and control.

Personal Growth: A crucial aspect of the *will-to-power* is the idea of self-overcoming. This involves a continuous process of challenging oneself, pushing beyond one's limits, and striving for personal excellence. It's not simply about external power or domination over others, but also about internal growth and transformation. Nietzsche believed that true fulfilment comes from this dynamic process of self-improvement and overcoming internal and external obstacles.

The Will-to-Power in these Lyrics
In the lyrics, we observe a narrative of personal transformation and self-enhancement, which aligns with Nietzsche's idea of the will to power. The speaker describes how they met the person when she was working as a waitress in a cocktail bar and how they played a pivotal role in transforming her life (*turned you into someone new*). This transformation can be seen as an expression of the *will-to-power*, where the individual goes beyond their initial state and strives for a higher form of existence, achieving significant success (*Now five years later on you've got the world at your feet*).

The dynamics of power and influence in the lyrics also reflect Nietzsche's concept. The speaker asserts their role in the other person's success, emphasising that it was their influence that facilitated her rise (*don't forget it's me who put you where you are now*). This highlights the speaker's exertion of power over the other person, both in their rise and the implicit threat of being able to bring them down (*And I can put you back down too*). Nietzsche's idea of the *will-to-power* encompasses not just personal growth and overcoming but also the exertion of influence and control over others.

The narrative in the lyrics can be interpreted as a journey of self-overcoming for the waitress-turned-successful individual. Her initial state of working in a cocktail bar contrasts sharply with her later success, symbolising a significant personal evolution and enhancement of her capabilities and status. Nietzsche's concept of self-overcoming is evident here as she transcends her previous limitations and achieves a higher state of being, embodying the drive for excellence. Nietzsche's concept of self-overcoming, or

"Selbstüberwindung" in German, is a central theme in his philosophy that pertains to the continual process of personal growth, transformation, and overcoming one's limitations. Self-overcoming is ultimately an affirmation of life and the inherent potential for growth and development. Through self-overcoming, individuals can cultivate a sense of purpose, meaning, and vitality in their lives, transcending the limitations imposed by external circumstances or societal norms.

Nietzsche emphasised that the *will-to-power* is about the desire for self-mastery and realising one's potential. The waitress's journey from working in a cocktail bar to having *'the world at your feet'* embodies this idea. Her success is an example of self-overcoming and reaching new heights, which Nietzsche viewed as a fundamental human drive. The lyrics highlight how she has managed to assert herself and achieve significant personal growth and accomplishment, thus realising her potential. The speaker's narrative also underscores Nietzsche's belief that individuals are inherently motivated to assert themselves and overcome challenges. The waitress's transformation is a testament to her inner drive to surpass her previous limitations and achieve success.

The song's narrative also prompts a reflection on the nature of influence and power. The speaker's claim to have *'picked you out, I shook you up'* and transformed the other person's life underscores a dynamic where one individual's *will-to-power* significantly impacts another's trajectory. This reflects Nietzsche's understanding of the complex interplay of *will-to-power* in human relationships, where one's drive for enhancement and influence can deeply affect another's path to self-overcoming. Central to Nietzsche's understanding of human relationships is the idea of conflict and competition. He believed that individuals are inherently in competition with one another, vying for dominance and recognition.

This competition arises from the drive for power and self-affirmation, leading to struggles for superiority and status. The assertion *"it's me who put you where you are now"* reflects an interplay of *wills-to-power*, where the speaker's actions facilitated her journey towards self-realisation and mastery. While Nietzsche acknowledged that relationships can foster mutual growth, he also recognised that the *will-to-power* often manifests as a struggle for dominance. Similarly, the song's narrative suggests that the waitress's transformation, while beneficial to her, also serves to affirm the speaker's superiority in shaping her success. This dynamic reflects Nietzsche's view that self-affirmation can emerge not only from empowerment but also from the assertion of influence over others."

Nietzsche was highly critical of traditional moral systems, particularly those based on Judeo-Christian values, which he believed were designed to suppress the *will-to-power* and enforce conformity. In the lyrics, we see a transformative journey where the waitress moves from a position of relative powerlessness to one of success and autonomy. This transformation can be viewed as a rebellion against traditional roles and expectations, which aligns with Nietzsche's desire to challenge and overturn restrictive moral norms. Nietzsche argued that traditional morality enforces conformity and stifles individuality The waitress's initial role in a cocktail bar could be seen as emblematic of a conformist and suppressed state, where her potential and inherent drives are not fully realised. The speaker's influence helps her break free from this state, suggesting a shift from suppression to the expression of her inherent drives, consistent with Nietzsche's critique. The transformation she undergoes signifies the unleashing of her *will-to-power*, striving for self-mastery and excellence beyond societal constraints.

The waitress's journey from working in a cocktail bar to achieving significant success reflects a narrative of overcoming adversity. This transformation illustrates the Nietzschean idea that challenges and hardships are not merely obstacles but necessary conditions for personal growth and the expression of the will to power. Nietzsche believed that personal growth is achieved through the struggle and conflict inherent in life. The lyrics suggest that the waitress's success was not handed to her without effort; rather, it was the result of a process that involved significant personal change and development (*I picked you out, I shook you up, and turned you around*). This narrative aligns with Nietzsche's view that enduring and overcoming difficulties is integral to achieving greater heights and realising one's potential.

The lyrics provide a vivid illustration of Nietzsche's concept of the *will-to-power*, capturing themes of personal transformation, self-overcoming, and the dynamics of influence. The lyrics echo Nietzsche's belief that life's adversities and the exertion of influence are not merely to be overcome but are integral to the process of becoming and self-realisation. The story of the waitress's transformation captures the essence of Nietzschean thought i.e. the relentless drive for self-enhancement, the importance of struggle in personal growth, and the intricate power dynamics that define human relationships.

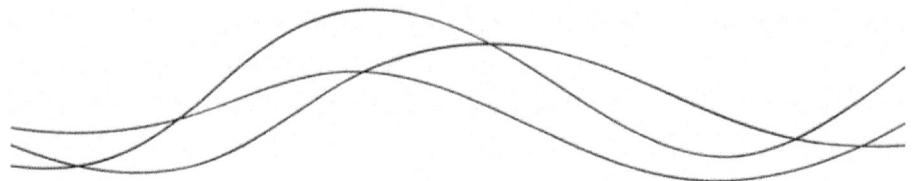

Kenny Loggins

Footloose

You're playing so cool
Obeying every rule
Deep way down in your heart
You're burning, yearning for some
Somebody to tell you
That life ain't passing you by
I'm trying to tell you
It will if you don't even try

Bad Faith

Jean-Paul Sartre, a French philosopher and a leading figure in existentialism, emphasised the idea of radical freedom and the profound responsibility that accompanies it. In his seminal work *Being and Nothingness*, he introduces the concept of *mauvaise foi*, or *bad faith*, a form of self-deception in which individuals deny or obscure their own freedom to avoid the anxiety that comes with it. *Bad faith* occurs when a person convinces themselves that their identity and circumstances are fixed, predetermined, or dictated by external forces such as society, culture, or fate. Instead of embracing their autonomy, they surrender to social roles and expectations, seeking comfort in the illusion that they have no real choice.

A classic example Sartre provides is that of a waiter who performs his duties with exaggerated precision and enthusiasm, as if he were nothing more than a waiter, reducing himself to a rigid social function rather than a conscious, free being. Another example is a person who, in a moment of temptation, refuses to acknowledge their desires, convincing themselves that they are not the kind of person who would act on them. In both cases, the individual avoids true self-awareness by identifying completely with a predefined role or by denying aspects of their own nature. This self-deception serves as a psychological defence mechanism, shielding them from the weight of responsibility that comes with acknowledging their freedom.

Closely linked to bad faith is Sartre's notion that human beings are *condemned to be free*. This phrase captures the paradoxical nature of human existence: while freedom is often considered an ideal, Sartre argues that it is also an inescapable burden. Unlike objects, which simply exist without question, human beings must actively define themselves through their choices. There is no inherent essence or purpose that dictates what a person should be, instead, each individual must forge their own identity and values through conscious action. However, this limitless freedom comes with a profound existential anxiety, as there are no absolute guidelines, external authorities, or predetermined meanings to rely on.

This existential burden is most apparent in moments of crisis, when individuals must make difficult choices that shape the course of their lives. Sartre argues that people often try to escape this responsibility by deferring to external authorities, traditions, or moral codes, believing that these forces can absolve them of the need to choose for themselves. For example, someone might claim that societal norms or their upbringing have determined their career path, romantic choices, or ethical beliefs, rather than acknowledging that they have actively chosen to conform to these influences. This self-imposed limitation, though comforting, is an illusion, as even the act of submission is itself a choice, one that reinforces bad faith.

Sartre insists that true authenticity requires individuals to confront their freedom directly, embracing the anxiety and responsibility that come with it. Instead of allowing external pressures to dictate their actions, individuals must recognise that they alone are responsible for shaping their identity and values. This does not mean acting impulsively or rejecting all social norms, but rather making choices with full awareness of their significance. In doing so, a person moves beyond b*ad faith* and into a state of authentic existence, where they take full ownership of their decisions and accept the consequences of their freedom.

In Sartre's view, this confrontation with freedom is not a one-time event but an ongoing process. Since human beings are constantly evolving, they must continuously reassess their choices, ensuring that they are living in alignment with their true selves rather than falling back into self-deception. Authenticity, therefore, is not a static state but a lifelong commitment to self-awareness and responsibility.

Bad Faith in these Lyrics
The lyrics call to break free from conformity and embrace life resonates with Sartre's emphasis on individual agency and the need to take responsibility for one's existence. Sartre's existentialist philosophy promotes the idea that individuals should actively engage with life, make meaningful choices, and define their own essence through their actions.

The lyrics convey a message of encouragement and empowerment. The speaker is urging the listener to recognise their inherent freedom and agency in shaping their own life. They're reminding them that *life will pass them by* if they remain passive and complacent, emphasising the importance of taking initiative and seizing opportunities. individuals have the power to transcend societal expectations and pursue their own path. It challenges the listener to break free from conformity and embrace their autonomy, reminding them that they have the freedom to define their own destiny.

These lyrics also suggest a tension between outward conformity and an inner desire for liberation and authenticity. The notion of *playing so cool* and *obeying every rule* is indicative of a conformist attitude. Despite outward conformity, there's an inner longing and dissatisfaction expressed in the lyrics. The person is described as *burning, yearning* for something more, suggesting a desire for deeper fulfilment or meaning beyond mere obedience to rules. By obediently following rules and seeking external validation, the individual denies their inherent freedom and agency in shaping their own destiny.

They may believe that conforming to societal norms will bring them fulfilment or validation, but in reality, they are sacrificing their authenticity and autonomy in the process. Sartre might interpret this tension as a manifestation of *bad faith*. The individual in the lyrics seems to be adhering to external norms and rules, seeking validation or reassurance from others. However, the lyrics also present a call to action, urging the individual to break free from this conformist pattern *You'll get by if you'd only cut loose.*

Authenticity, a key theme in existentialism, is about living in accordance with one's true self, values, and choices. Cutting loose means striving for authenticity by rejecting the inauthentic roles and behaviours that may be adopted in bad faith. It entails the courage to be true to oneself despite societal expectations. The individual's yearning for validation and reassurance suggests a deeper search for meaning and authenticity in their life. Cutting loose involves embracing the uncertainty of life and taking risks. Sartre emphasised that the future is not predetermined, and individuals must create their own meaning through their choices. Rejecting bad faith means stepping into the unknown, facing existential anxiety, and actively engaging with the possibilities that freedom offers.

Existentialists, like Jean-Paul Sartre, often viewed anxiety not only as a source of discomfort but also as a powerful catalyst for action and personal growth. The call to *cut loose* can also be seen as an acknowledgment of anxiety as a natural part of the human condition and a challenge to use that anxiety as motivation to break free from conformity and pursue a more authentic life. Existential anxiety arises from the recognition of our freedom and the inherent uncertainty of life. Cutting loose requires confronting this anxiety head-on, understanding that it is a natural part of the human condition, and using it as a catalyst for authentic living rather than succumbing to self-deceptive practices.

Existential anxiety often arises when individuals confront the unknown or uncertain aspects of life. The lyrics suggest that the person addressed is *burning, yearning for some*, indicating a deep desire for something more meaningful or fulfilling. This yearning can evoke anxiety as it involves stepping into the unknown and challenging the familiar. The lyrics emphasise the urgency of life and the potential for it to pass by if the individual doesn't take action. Existential anxiety may manifest as a fear of missed opportunities, a sense of time slipping away, or an awareness of the transient nature of life. The call to *cut loose* suggests a response to this fear by actively engaging with life. Existential anxiety is often intertwined with the recognition of radical freedom and the corresponding responsibility to shape one's own destiny. The person in the lyrics may experience anxiety when faced with the responsibility of making choices that will define their existence. The call to *cut loose* encourages a proactive response to this existential anxiety.

These lyrics encapsulate core themes of Jean-Paul Sartre's existentialist philosophy, particularly the emphasis on individual freedom, authenticity, and the rejection of conformity. By challenging the listener to embrace their freedom and confront the uncertainties of life, the song encourages a journey toward authenticity, personal growth, and a deeper understanding of one's own existence.

Huey Lewis and the News

The Power of Love

*Don't need money, don't take fame
Don't need no credit card to ride this train
It's strong and it's sudden and it's cruel sometimes
But it might just save your life
That's the power of love*

The rejection of money, fame, and the need for a credit card to experience the *power of love* can be seen as a commentary on materialism and consumerism. Philosophers like Karl Marx and the Frankfurt School, including thinkers like Herbert Marcuse, critiqued the commodification of relationships and the impact of consumer culture on human experience

Commodification of Relationships
In a capitalist system, labour itself becomes a commodity. Workers sell their labour power in exchange for wages, which alienates them from the products of their labour and from their own human potential. This alienation extends to personal relationships, as individuals start to view each other through the lens of economic value. Social interactions are increasingly mediated by money and market transactions. Marx argued that capitalism inherently leads to the commodification of various aspects of life because of its focus on profit maximisation and the accumulation of capital.

Commodity fetishism refers to the way commodities are endowed with social power and value that appear to be inherent in the commodities themselves, rather than being a result of the social relationships and labour that produced them. Commodity fetishism involves an inversion where the social relationships between people (e.g. between workers and capitalists) are masked by the relationships between commodities. The products of labour appear to have value on their own, divorced from the labour that created them. commodities are treated as if they possess a life and value of their own. This reification, or *"thingification"* of social relations leads people to see commodities as natural objects with intrinsic value, rather than as products of human labour.

This process contributes to the alienation of workers, who do not see the true value of their labour reflected in the commodities they produce. Instead, they see the commodity as something alien and external, possessing value independently. The fetishism of commodities creates the illusion that the market and economic relations operate independently of human agency. This masks the exploitative relationships and power dynamics inherent in capitalist production. People begin to perceive social relations and their own identities through the prism of commodities and their exchange values. This influences how individuals see themselves and others, often valuing people based on their possessions and consumption patterns. In contemporary society, branded goods and consumer products are often fetishised. For instance, a brand-name sneaker is valued not just for its utility but for the social status it confers on its owner.

Marx's analysis suggests that the intrusion of market logic into personal spheres is a symptom of broader capitalist dynamics. This can lead to a superficial valuation of relationships based on economic benefits rather than genuine personal connections. Platforms like Tinder or Match.com turn romantic relationships into a form of market exchange, where potential partners are selected and evaluated based on profiles, much like products. Relationships on social media can become commodified through the monetisation of personal connections, followers, and likes, transforming social interactions into marketable assets.

Marx also argued that capitalism creates *false needs*, desires for goods and services that are not essential to human well-being but are generated by the capitalist system to sustain consumption and profit. Advertising and marketing in consumer culture create and perpetuate false needs, making individuals believe that their happiness and self-worth depend on the continuous acquisition of new products. This leads to a cycle of consumption that prioritises material goods over true human needs and fulfilment.

Consumer culture encourages individuals to form relationships based on consumption patterns and brand affiliations rather than genuine human connections. This undermines community and solidarity, as people are driven to compete for status through consumption rather than collaborate to address common needs and goals. The relentless pursuit of profit and the creation of false needs drive overproduction and overconsumption, leading to environmental degradation. By promoting constant consumption, consumer culture contributes to unsustainable practices that harm the environment and, by extension, human well-being.

Commodification of Relationships in these Lyrics

The lyrics *Don't need money, don't take fame / Don't need no credit card to ride this train*, suggest that love is an authentic human experience that cannot be bought or sold, aligning with Marx's vision of uncommodified human interactions. Marx emphasised the importance of genuine human relationships that are not mediated by economic concerns. The idea that love *might just save your life* suggests that authentic human connections have profound, life-affirming value that cannot be replicated by material goods or financial transactions. Marx believed that capitalist society alienates individuals from their labour, the products they produce, and from each other. This alienation extends to personal relationships, which can become superficial and transactional. The song's emphasis on love as a powerful, life-saving force speaks to the deep, authentic connections that Marx envisioned in a society free from alienation and commodification.

The idea that love doesn't require money or fame reinforces the notion that its true value lies in its authenticity, which is not subject to the distortions of a market economy. Marx believed that capitalism alienates individuals from their true selves and from each other, reducing social interactions to economic exchanges. By emphasising that love operates outside the realm of economic transactions, the lyrics present an ideal where human connections are pure and unaffected by material concerns. This reflects a desire for relationships based on mutual affection and solidarity rather than economic benefit.

The repeated emphasis on love's independence from money and fame, (*Don't need money, don't take fame*) resonates with Marx's critique by suggesting that love meets a fundamental human need that is not a product of capitalist manipulation. Love transcends material wealth and economic transactions. The song asserts that love's true power lies in its freedom from these market-driven valuations. It presents an ideal where human experiences are valued for their intrinsic qualities rather than their economic worth. This emphasis on love's independence from money and fame underscores a rejection of the false needs created by consumer culture. Marx argued that capitalism generates false needs to drive consumption, diverting people from their true human needs.

The lyrics celebrate love as an essential, humanising force, emphasising that it is a profound aspect of life. By emphasising that love cannot be bought or sold, the song underscores the importance of humanising relationships. It suggests that love retains its value and meaning precisely because it resists commodification and remains an authentic human experience. The lyrics *Don't need no credit card to ride this train* imply that love and meaningful connections exist outside the realm of economic transactions. The metaphor of a *train* that doesn't require a *credit card* suggests a journey or experience that is accessible to everyone, regardless of financial status.

The lyrics suggest a form of liberation from the constraints of a capitalist society that values wealth and fame. Marx envisioned a society where individuals could overcome the alienation and exploitation associated with capitalism. The idea that love has the power to save lives might be interpreted as a way to escape or resist the negative aspects of capitalist structures.

The song's lyrics emphasise love as an authentic, uncommodified human experience that transcends money and fame, aligning with Marx's critique of capitalism's tendency to reduce relationships to economic transactions. Marx viewed capitalism as a system that alienates individuals from their labour, products, and each other, turning social interactions into market exchanges. The song counters this by portraying love as a powerful, humanising force that resists commodification, offering a vision of relationships rooted in mutual affection rather than economic benefit. Through this lens, the lyrics symbolise liberation from capitalist constraints, affirming that true fulfilment lies in non-material values rather than consumer culture's false needs.

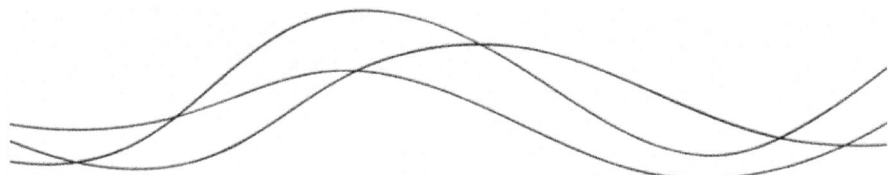

Madonna

Material Girl

Some boys try, and some boys lie
But I don't let them play (no way)
Only boys that save their pennies
Make my rainy day

This portrayal of superficiality and materialism resonates with the concept of the *Iron Cage of Rationality* offered by the German philosopher, Max Weber. Weber described how rationalisation, the process of replacing traditional, emotional, or value-driven modes of thinking and behaviours with rational and calculated ones, has become increasingly pervasive in modern society.

The Iron Cage of Rationality
In the context of bureaucracy, Weber argued that rationalisation has led to the creation of systems and structures that prioritise efficiency, predictability, and control. While this has benefits such as increased productivity and organisation, it also has drawbacks. The *iron cage* metaphorically represents the restrictive and confining nature of these rationalised structures.

In the *iron cage of rationality*, individuals and organisations become trapped in systems that prioritise rules, procedures, and impersonal relationships over human needs and values. Decisions are often made based on calculative logic rather than empathy or intuition. This can lead to alienation, disenchantment, and a sense of powerlessness among individuals as they navigate bureaucratic institutions.

Weber's concept of the *Disenchantment of the World* refers to the idea that as societies modernise and rationalise, they undergo a transformation in their worldview, moving away from traditional, mystical, or religious beliefs towards a more rational and scientific understanding of the world. In pre-modern societies, beliefs in spirits, gods, magic, and the supernatural often dominated people's understanding of the world. These beliefs provided explanations for natural phenomena, guided social norms and behaviours, and offered a sense of meaning and purpose to individuals and communities.

However, with the rise of modernity and the spread of scientific thought, these traditional beliefs gradually lost their authority and influence. Rationalisation, characterised by the application of reason, logic, and systematic procedures, became increasingly dominant in various aspects of society, including politics, economics, and culture. Weber argued that as societies embraced rationalisation and scientific thinking, they experienced a *disenchantment* of the world. This *disenchantment* refers to the stripping away of the mystical, magical, and spiritual elements from people's understanding of the world. Natural phenomena were no longer attributed to divine intervention or supernatural forces but were instead explained through empirical observation, experimentation, and scientific laws.

The *disenchantment of the world* has significant implications for individuals and societies. On one hand, it leads to the decline of traditional religious and metaphysical beliefs, which can result in feelings of existential uncertainty, loss of meaning, and a sense of alienation for some individuals. On the other hand, it fosters the development of a more rational, empirical, and potentially progressive worldview, laying the groundwork for scientific advancement, technological innovation, and social change.

The Iron Cage of Rationality in these Lyrics

The portrayal of valuing boys for their wealth reflects this rationalised approach to relationships, where material gain becomes a primary consideration. In a rationalised society, relationships, like other social interactions, become more transactional and calculative. The lyrics *Only boys that save their pennies / Make my rainy day* suggest that she evaluates potential partners based on their financial stability and ability to save money, reflecting a calculative and pragmatic approach to relationships.

The lyrics imply a preference for efficiency in choosing partners, valuing those who are economically prudent (*Only boys that save their pennies*). This mirrors Weber's notion of *rationalisation*, where efficiency becomes a key criterion in various aspects of life, including personal relationships. The emphasis on *boys that save their pennies* highlights calculability, a core element of rationalisation. The protagonist assesses partners based on their financial habits, akin to evaluating the predictability and reliability of their economic behaviour.

By setting clear criteria for partner selection based on financial behaviour, the protagonist exercises control over their social interactions. This reflects the rationalised approach where control is maintained through standardised criteria and predictable outcomes. The focus on financial prudence ensures a predictable and stable relationship, minimising the risks associated with financial instability. This mirrors Weber's idea that rationalisation aims to reduce unpredictability in social and economic life.

The lyrics reflect a disenchantment with romantic ideals, replacing them with a pragmatic, rational approach to relationships. This echoes Weber's notion of disenchantment, where traditional values and emotional connections are overshadowed by rational, calculative thinking. The protagonist's criteria for partner selection is a clear example of instrumental rationality, where relationships are approached with a means-end calculation. The *pennies* saved by potential partners are seen as a means to ensure financial security and stability.

In the *Iron Cage of Rationality*, individuals and societies become trapped in systems where rational calculation, efficiency, and the pursuit of material gain dominate. The lyrics *Some boys try, and some boys lie, But I don't let them play* echoes the rational mindset of prioritising one's own interests and being selective in relationships to ensure personal benefit, which is characteristic of the rationalised systems described by Max Weber. These lyrics reflect a pragmatic and self-interested attitude, emphasising material gain and personal advantage over traditional notions of love or companionship. This prioritisation of material wealth over emotional or spiritual connection mirrors the shift away from traditional values towards a more rational and self-interested worldview characteristic of the disenchantment process.

Essentially, these lyrics are emblematic of the disenchantment of the world, portraying a society where materialism and self-interest have replaced traditional values and beliefs, reflecting the broader cultural shifts associated with modernisation and rationalisation.

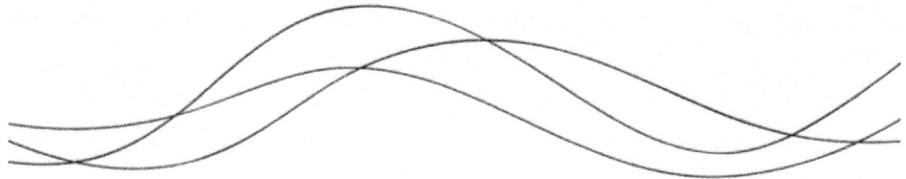

Eurythmics

Sweet Dreams

Some of them want to use you
Some of them want to get used by you
Some of them want to abuse you
Some of them want to be abused

The lyrics suggest a range of desires and power dynamics within interpersonal relationships. The lyrics can be viewed within the framework of Sigmund Freud's structural model of the psyche, which consists of three components: the id, ego, and superego. Each of these psychological structures plays a role in shaping human behaviour and desires.

Sigmund Freud's Structural Model of the Psyche
The *id* is the most primitive and instinctual part of the psyche. It operates on the pleasure principle, seeking immediate gratification of basic needs and desires. The *id* is impulsive, unconscious, and not bound by rationality or morality. It represents innate drives, such as hunger, thirst, and sexual impulses. The *id* provides the psychic energy needed for psychological processes but lacks the ability to distinguish between reality and fantasy. It seeks immediate gratification of basic biological needs and desires, such as hunger, thirst, and sexual impulses, without regard for consequences or morality.

The *id* operates largely at an unconscious level, motivating individuals to seek pleasure and avoid pain without rational consideration. It is driven by primary processes of wish fulfilment, shaping individuals' thoughts, feelings, and behaviours from a primal and instinctual perspective. The *id's* desires are impulsive and irrational, often leading individuals to act on instinctual impulses without considering the long-term consequences. It represents the raw, unfiltered aspects of human nature, operating without inhibition or restraint.

The *ego* emerges as a response to the external world. It operates on the reality principle, aiming to satisfy the *id's* desires in a way that is realistic and socially acceptable. The *ego* is rational, conscious, and considers consequences. It engages in problem-solving and decision-making, mediating between the demands of the *id* and the constraints of the external environment. The *ego* helps individuals adapt to the external world, navigating challenges and finding realistic ways to fulfil desires.

The *ego* emerges from the *id* during infancy and represents the rational and conscious part of the psyche. It operates on the reality principle, seeking to satisfy the desires of the *id* in socially acceptable ways while considering the constraints of reality, morality, and practicality. The *ego* acts as a mediator between the demands of the id and the constraints of reality, striving to maintain psychological equilibrium and meet the individual's needs. Unlike the *id*, which operates largely at an unconscious level, the *ego* enables individuals to consider the consequences of their actions and make choices based on rational considerations.

The *superego* develops during early childhood through the internalisation of societal and parental values. It represents the moral and ethical standards of society. The *superego* incorporates a sense of right and wrong, and it enforces moral judgments. It can lead to feelings of guilt, shame, or pride based on adherence to, or violation of societal norms. The *superego* acts as a guiding force, influencing behaviour by imposing moral constraints and ideals. It consists of two components, the conscience, which punishes the individual for violating moral standards, and the *ego-ideal*, which rewards the individual for meeting moral expectations.

The *superego* operates at both conscious and unconscious levels, exerting moral and ethical control over the individual's thoughts, feelings, and behaviours. It guides individuals to adhere to societal norms and values, shaping their perceptions of right and wrong. The *superego* embodies the individual's idealised self-image and aspirations, influencing their aspirations and behaviours.

Struggles between these psychic structures manifest as psychological tension and contribute to various aspects of human behaviour. The *ego* serves as a mediator between the conflicting demands of the id, which seeks immediate gratification, and the *superego*, which imposes moral and societal constraints. The *ego* must balance these competing demands while navigating the external environment, often employing defence mechanisms to cope with internal conflicts and reduce anxiety.

Conflict and tension may arise as individuals navigate the competing demands of the *id, ego,* and *superego*. Internal conflicts between instinctual desires and moral considerations can lead to psychological distress and emotional turmoil, requiring resolution through compromise, adaptation, or defence mechanisms.

Structural Model of the Psyche in these Lyrics
In these lyrics, the desire to *use* or *get used* could be seen as expressions of the *id's* primal urges for pleasure without much consideration for moral or social norms. The *id* is often associated with unconscious and impulsive drives. The *id*-driven desires for immediate pleasure (use, get used) may conflict with the more rational considerations of the *ego*. The lyrics evoke

themes of desire, manipulation, and exploitation in interpersonal relationships, reflecting the *id's* impulsive and instinctual drives. Some individuals may seek to use others for their own gratification, while others may willingly submit to being used or even desire to be mistreated or abused. These desires and behaviours can stem from unconscious impulses and drives associated with the *id*, driving individuals to seek pleasure and fulfilment through various means, even if they are harmful or self-destructive.

The *id* operates without a sense of morality or consideration for the consequences of its actions. In the lyrics, individuals may act on primal urges and desires without regard for the ethical or moral implications of their behaviour. This lack of moral restraint can lead to exploitation, manipulation, and abuse in relationships, as individuals prioritise their own immediate needs and desires over the well-being of others.

In the lyrics, the *ego* might come into play as individuals negotiate and balance their desires for use, being used, abuse, or being abused within the context of social and relational realities. The negotiation between the *id's* impulses and the external world's demands could result in different relationship dynamics. The *ego's* function of mediating between the *id* and *superego* can be seen in the lyric's depiction of individuals with varying desires and intentions.

The *ego* must navigate the conflicting desires of those who seek to use or be used by others, balancing the pursuit of pleasure with considerations of social norms and personal integrity. Freud described the *ego* as operating on the reality principle, meaning it evaluates the external world and adapts behaviour to meet the demands of reality. In the context of the lyrics, the *ego* may engage in reality testing by assessing the intentions and motivations of others, discerning between genuine connections and manipulative relationships. The *ego* employs defence mechanisms to protect the individual from distressing thoughts, feelings, or impulses arising from conflicts between the *id* and *superego*. In the lyrics, individuals may use defence mechanisms such as denial, rationalisation, or projection to cope with the complexities of interpersonal relationships and avoid confronting uncomfortable truths.

The desire to *abuse* or *be abused* could be seen as conflicts with societal norms, potentially leading to moral dilemmas and internal struggles governed by the *superego*. The lyrics depict individuals with varying desires and intentions in relationships, suggesting a complex interplay between personal motivations and moral standards. The *superego*, representing internalised societal norms and values, influences individuals' behaviour by dictating what is considered morally right or wrong. In navigating these interpersonal dynamics, individuals may be guided by the moral imperatives of the *superego*, seeking to align their actions with societal expectations and avoid behaviours perceived as morally reprehensible.

The lyrics portray a spectrum of desires, from those who seek to use or abuse others to those who desire to be used or abused. Individuals may navigate these power dynamics and assert boundaries in relationships according to the moral standards imposed by the *superego*, seeking to maintain integrity and uphold ethical principles in their interactions.

Conflicts between personal desires and moral considerations are evident in the lyrics, reflecting the tension between the *id's* instinctual drives and the *superego's* moral imperatives. Individuals may experience internal conflict and psychological distress when their actions deviate from the moral standards imposed by the *superego*, leading to feelings of guilt, shame, or ambivalence. Resolving these conflicts requires reconciling personal motivations with the moral expectations of the superego, seeking to uphold ethical principles and values in relationships and interactions.

These lyrics vividly illustrate Freud's structural model by highlighting the intricate interplay between the *id, ego,* and *superego* in shaping human behaviour. The narrative reflects the ongoing internal conflicts that arise as individuals navigate their desires, reality, and moral conscience within the realm of human relationships. These dynamic underscores the enduring relevance of Freud's insights into the complexities of the human psyche and the challenges of balancing instinctual drives with ethical considerations.

Foreigner

I Want to Know What Love Is

In my life, there's been heartache and pain
I don't know if I can face it again
Can't stop now, I've travelled so far
To change this lonely life

The lyrics evoke themes of resilience, perseverance, and existential struggle, which can be linked to the philosophical ideas of Friedrich Nietzsche, particularly his concept of *Eternal Recurrence* and the notion of overcoming adversity to create meaning in life.

Eternal Recurrence
Nietzsche's concept of Eternal Recurrence, is a philosophical idea that suggests the universe and all events within it are eternally recurring in a cycle, repeating themselves infinitely across time. This concept is one of Nietzsche's most profound and challenging thoughts, and it carries significant existential implications.

Nietzsche presents *Eternal Recurrence* as a thought experiment in his work *The Gay Science* and elaborates on it in *Thus Spoke Zarathustra*. He asks us to imagine that our lives, with all their events, joys and sorrow, will recur infinitely, without any changes, in exactly the same sequence. The idea of *Eternal Recurrence* poses a profound existential challenge. It asks individuals to reflect on their lives and decisions with the understanding that they will relive every moment eternally. This thought forces one to consider whether they are living a life they would be willing to repeat forever.

Nietzsche saw *Eternal Recurrence* as a way to overcome *nihilism*, the belief that life is meaningless. By embracing the idea that every moment is eternally significant, individuals can find purpose and value in their actions and experiences. The notion of *Eternal Recurrence* can have a profound psychological impact, compelling individuals to revaluate their values, priorities, and actions. It challenges people to live authentically and meaningfully, knowing that their choices hold eternal weight.

Nietzsche believed that the individual's ability to overcome adversity and affirm life's hardships is central to the creation of meaning and fulfilment. This statement encapsulates a core aspect of Nietzsche's philosophy, emphasising resilience and the embrace of life's challenges as essential components of a meaningful existence. Nietzsche often wrote about the importance of facing and overcoming difficulties. He believed that personal growth and strength emerge through the struggle against obstacles. This idea is famously captured in his phrase '*What does not kill me makes me stronger*'. By confronting and surmounting hardships, individuals develop their character, resilience, and capacity for self-overcoming.

Nietzsche argued that one should not merely endure suffering but affirm it as an integral part of life. This means accepting and embracing life's pain and difficulties as necessary for growth and authenticity. He introduced the concept of *amor fati* (love of fate), which encourages individuals to love their life in its entirety, including its suffering and setbacks, as these are what make life complete and meaningful. For Nietzsche, meaning and fulfilment are not given but created through one's actions and choices. By overcoming adversity and affirming life's hardships, individuals actively participate in shaping their destiny and imbuing their lives with purpose. Nietzsche believed that true fulfilment arises from living authentically and fully embracing all aspects of existence. This includes not only the joyful and pleasurable moments but also the painful and challenging ones. By doing so, individuals transcend mere survival and achieve a deeper sense of fulfilment that comes from living in accordance with their values and aspirations.

Eternal Recurrence in these Lyrics

The lyrics *In my life, there's been heartache and pain / I don't know if I can face it again*, immediately evoke themes of struggle and adversity. This sentiment aligns closely with Nietzsche's philosophy, particularly his concept of *Eternal Recurrence* and the necessity of overcoming hardship to create meaning in life. The lyrics reflect a moment of existential crisis, where the singer acknowledges their pain and questions their ability to persist, mirroring Nietzsche's view that true strength emerges from confronting life's difficulties.

The idea of perseverance is reinforced in the lines, *Can't stop now, I've travelled so far / To change this lonely life*. Here, the singer expresses a determination to move forward despite past suffering. This embodies Nietzsche's notion of *self-overcoming*, the process of transforming pain and adversity into personal growth, echoing the statement '*What does not kill me makes me stronger*'. The lyrics mirror this sentiment, portraying an individual who, despite hardship, chooses to continue their journey rather than succumb to despair.

The *phrase I don't know if I can face it again* can be interpreted as an existential question, whether the individual can bear the weight of recurring pain. Nietzsche's concept of *Eternal Recurrence* proposed that one should live in such a way that they would be willing to relive their life, with all its struggles, infinitely and would argue that true strength lies in affirming life in its entirety, including its hardships. The resolve to keep moving forward, as expressed in *Can't stop now*, suggests an unconscious embrace of this challenge, an implicit acceptance of Nietzsche's *amor fati*, or love of fate.

Additionally, Nietzsche believed that meaning is not given but created. The lyrics imply a desire for transformation (*To change this lonely life*), which reflects Nietzsche's belief in the individual's power to shape their own destiny. By actively seeking change rather than resigning to suffering, the singer embodies the Nietzschean ideal of forging meaning through struggle. This aligns with Nietzsche's view that life's purpose is not found in external validation but in one's ability to overcome obstacles and affirm existence on their own terms.

These lyrics capture key elements of Nietzsche's philosophy, including the necessity of overcoming adversity, the idea of *Eternal Recurrence,* and the creation of meaning through struggle. The singer acknowledges suffering but refuses to surrender to it, embodying Nietzsche's belief that true strength and fulfilment arise from embracing life's challenges. By choosing to persist and transform their circumstances, they exemplify the Nietzschean ideal of self-overcoming and the affirmation of life in all its aspects.

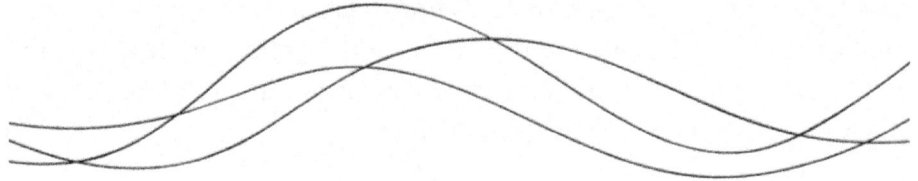

Journey

Don't Stop Believin'

Strangers waitin'
Up and down the boulevard
Their shadows searchin' in the night
Streetlights, people
Livin' just to find emotion
Hidin', somewhere in the night

These lyrics evoke a sense of urban loneliness, existential searching, and the quest for meaning amidst the anonymity of the cityscape. Heidegger, a German existentialist philosopher, explored themes of urban loneliness and existential searching within the concept of *being-in-the-world*.

Being-in-the-World
The concept of *being-in-the-world* is a central idea in Heidegger's book *Being and Time*. This concept represents Heidegger's attempt to understand human existence (or *Dasein*, as he terms it) in its most fundamental sense, emphasising the interconnectedness between humans and their environment Heidegger argues that humans do not exist in isolation but are always already situated within a world, which he terms *being-in-the-world*. This concept suggests that human existence is inherently relational, with individuals always being in a particular context or environment.

An example of *being-in-the-world* can be illustrated through the experience of a person taking a walk in a city park. When the person enters the park, they are immediately situated within a specific environment. The park provides a context with its trees, pathways, benches, and other features. As the person walks through the park, they encounter various elements of the environment, such as other people, animals, and natural scenery. Their experience is inherently relational, as they interact with these elements and are influenced by them. The person's experience of the park is mediated through their body. They feel the warmth of the sun on their skin, the texture of the grass under their feet, and the breeze rustling through the trees. *Being-in-the-world* emphasises the inseparable connection between humans and their surroundings. Humans do not merely exist as isolated individuals but are always engaged in relationships with other beings and objects in their environment. This interconnectedness shapes human experience and perception.

Heidegger's analysis of technology is particularly relevant to the urban context. He discusses how modern technology, while providing convenience and efficiency, can also contribute to a sense of alienation and estrangement from our authentic selves and the world around us. In urban settings, technology often mediates our interactions with others and shapes our experience of the environment, leading to a sense of detachment from our surroundings and from meaningful human connections. Instead of engaging directly with the world, we often interact through screens and interfaces, distancing ourselves from genuine human experiences and connections

Technology mediates our interactions with others in urban environments. Social media, messaging apps, and digital communication platforms have become ubiquitous tools for connecting with others. While these technologies enable instant communication and virtual interactions, they also shape the nature of our relationships. In many cases, these interactions lack the richness and depth of face-to-face communication, leading to a sense of detachment and superficiality in our social interactions.

Technology shapes our experience of the urban environment itself. From GPS navigation systems guiding our paths to augmented reality apps altering our perception of physical spaces, technology mediates how we perceive and interact with the world around us. This mediation can lead to a sense of detachment from our surroundings, as our attention becomes fragmented and our engagement with the physical environment becomes secondary to our digital experiences.

Heidegger's concept of *authenticity* encourages individuals to confront their own mortality and to embrace their existence as finite beings. In the face of urban loneliness and existential searching, Heidegger suggests that individuals can find meaning and authenticity by confronting their own mortality and by living authentically in accordance with their own values and beliefs. *Authenticity* requires an individual to take ownership of their existence, to live deliberately according to their own values rather than those imposed by external forces. This means embracing responsibility for one's choices, acting with genuine commitment, and recognizing that each moment of life is finite and therefore meaningful. In the context of modern urban loneliness and existential searching, Heidegger's philosophy suggests that meaning is not something passively discovered but actively created through engagement with one's own being. By facing mortality head-on and making conscious, self-determined choices, individuals can transcend the alienation of impersonal existence and cultivate a more profound sense of purpose and belonging.

Being-in-the-World in these Lyrics
The lyrics describe a city street, where people (*strangers*) move up and down, suggesting the bustling yet often impersonal nature of urban life. This resonates with Heidegger's idea that

individuals are not isolated but constantly situated in a relational context. The people waiting and moving along the boulevard are engaged with their surroundings and each other, even if only in passing. According to Heidegger, the body is the medium through which individuals interact with the world. The strangers walking up and down the boulevard represent the physical, embodied aspect of existence. Their movements and actions are ways of engaging with and experiencing the world around them

The lyrics *shadows searching in the night* suggests a quest for meaning or connection in a vast, possibly indifferent urban environment. This aligns with Heidegger's notion that human existence is always interconnected with the world around us. The presence of streetlights illuminating the night emphasises the connection between the urban infrastructure and human activity. The streetlights enable people to navigate and interact within the urban space, highlighting the interdependence between humans and their environment. This mirrors Heidegger's idea that surroundings shape human experience and perception. The interaction between streetlights and people underscores the temporality and transience of human life.

While streetlights provide visibility and safety, they also represent the pervasive presence of technology in urban life. According to Heidegger, this can lead to a superficial engagement with our surroundings, where we are constantly mediated by artificial light and other technological interfaces, distancing us from more direct, authentic interactions with the world. Streetlights provide momentary illumination in the darkness, symbolising the fleeting nature of human existence. Heidegger's focus on temporality involves the recognition that human life is finite and shaped by time.

Livin' Just to Find Emotion / Hidin', Somewhere in the Night suggest an emotional journey within the urban landscape, where people are searching for meaningful connections and experiences. The idea of hiding in the night underscores the complexity of human existence because it reflects themes of existential searching, alienation, and the tension between visibility and concealment in the urban landscape. Night often symbolises both freedom and anonymity, a space where individuals can either explore their true selves or retreat into obscurity. The act of hiding suggests an internal struggle, perhaps a fear of vulnerability, rejection, or existential uncertainty, implying that people navigate life not only seeking connection but also avoiding aspects of themselves or their reality. and the ongoing search for authenticity and emotional fulfilment.

This is connected to Heidegger's belief that humans are always in a state of involvement and engagement with the world, the environment, with its lights, streets, and the presence of other people, influences the emotional states and actions of the individuals. The emotions and actions of the people are not occurring in a vacuum but are deeply influenced by their urban context. Modern technology in urban environments makes life more convenient and efficient, however Heidegger warns that this convenience can alienate us from our authentic selves. The strangers on the boulevard, illuminated by streetlights, are part of an efficient system but may feel isolated and disconnected from genuine human experiences.

Heidegger's philosophy suggests that while modern conveniences enhance efficiency, they can also lead to alienation, mirroring the loneliness of the strangers on the boulevard, who remain part of the city's flow yet disconnected from deeper human experiences. This sense of alienation is compounded by the difficulty of achieving authenticity in a world that emphasises external roles and societal expectations over genuine self-expression. The strangers on the boulevard represent an inauthentic mode of existence, engaging with the world in a way that is shaped more by external forces than by an internal sense of self. Their movements, though part of the city's rhythm, lack deeper connection or reflection. Heidegger challenges individuals to break free from the superficial engagements of urban life and confront their mortality, freedom, and capacity for self-determined meaning.

The Police

Every Little Thing She Does Is Magic

But my silent fears have gripped me
Long before I reach the phone
Long before my tongue has tripped me
Must I always be alone

These lyrics express a profound sense of existential angst and the struggle with inner fears and loneliness. Søren Kierkegaard explored similar themes of anxiety, despair, and the individual's search for meaning and connection in a seemingly indifferent universe.

Existential Angst
One of Kierkegaard's central themes is *existential angst*, also referred to as *existential anxiety* or *dread*. Unlike ordinary fear, which arise from tangible dangers or external threats, *existential angst* stems from an individual's confrontation with the fundamental uncertainties of existence. It is an internal, deeply personal experience that emerges when one becomes aware of their own freedom, the weight of responsibility that accompanies it, and the absence of any predetermined meaning in life. At the core of Kierkegaard's existential thought is the idea that human beings possess absolute freedom to make choices. There is no external structure, whether societal, religious, or philosophical, that can provide ultimate certainty or remove this burden. Individuals must navigate life without a clear blueprint, and this lack of fixed guidance can lead to deep uncertainty. The realisation that life lacks inherent meaning, and that it is up to

each person to create their own values and purpose, often triggers *existential angst*. This anxiety is not simply an emotional response but an indication of a deeper existential truth, that human existence is characterised by an ongoing struggle between freedom and responsibility.

Kierkegaard described existential angst as an unavoidable part of human life, where each decision carries consequences that cannot be undone. He saw this anxiety as a double-edged sword, it can be paralysing, causing individuals to retreat into avoidance or despair, but it can also serve as a catalyst for growth and self-discovery. The fear of making the wrong choices, of failing to live authentically, or of wasting one's potential is a defining characteristic of human existence. However, rather than seeing this anxiety as something to be eliminated, Kierkegaard argued that it is essential to personal development. By facing this dread head-on, individuals have the opportunity to cultivate a deeper sense of purpose and meaning in their lives.

To navigate *existential angst*, Kierkegaard introduced the concept of the *leap-of-faith*. He believed that reason alone is insufficient for providing certainty or meaning, and that individuals must embrace life's uncertainties by making a passionate, committed choice. This leap is not a rejection of reason but an acknowledgment that rational thought has its limits, and that true meaning must be found through subjective experience. The *leap-of-faith* is an act of courage, requiring individuals to trust in something beyond logical proof, whether it be faith in God, a moral conviction, or a deeply held belief about the nature of existence. It is a way of transcending paralysing doubt and taking responsibility for shaping one's own life.

For Kierkegaard, the *leap-of-faith* represents the highest form of authentic living. Instead of being consumed by existential anxiety or falling into despair, individuals can choose to engage with life fully, embracing both its uncertainties and its possibilities. This does not mean escaping anxiety altogether, rather, transforming it into a driving force for personal growth. By confronting the fundamental uncertainties of existence and committing to a chosen path with passion and sincerity, individuals can move beyond fear and find deeper fulfilment. In this way, *existential angst* is not merely a burden but an essential aspect of what it means to live a meaningful life.

Existential Angst in these Lyrics

Kierkegaard emphasised the individual's quest for meaning and purpose in life, often explored through relationships and existential reflection. The lyrics expression of longing for connection and the fear of always being alone reflects the human desire for meaningful connections and the struggle to find solace amidst inner turmoil. The entire passage conveys a sense of searching and struggling with personal fears and isolation. This reflects the existential struggle, as the individual grapples with their silent fears and the feeling of being alone, searching for meaning and connection in a world that does not provide it inherently.

The lyrics, *But my silent fears have gripped me*, captures the essence of existential angst, which Kierkegaard describes as a profound, pervasive sense of anxiety or dread. The silent fears gripping the individual reflect the internal, overwhelming nature of *existential angst*. Questioning whether one must always be alone, ties into the recognition of one's absolute freedom and the responsibility to create meaning. This highlights the individual's struggle with fears and the quest for purpose in a life that lacks inherent meaning. Kierkegaard emphasises that individuals have the power to determine their own path in life, free from external constraints or predetermined outcomes. The lyrics resonate with this idea by portraying the speaker's inner struggles and fears, which arise from their awareness of this freedom. The line *But my silent fears have gripped me* suggests that despite having the freedom to act, the speaker feels trapped by their own anxieties. Kierkegaard considered anxiety as being inherent to human existence, stemming from our awareness of freedom and the responsibility it entails. The lyrics portrayal of silent fears gripping the speaker resonates deeply with this idea. The phrase *silent fears* suggests a profound, internalised sense of anxiety, echoing Kierkegaard's notion of existential dread.

Kierkegaard stressed the importance of authenticity and individual selfhood in navigating the existential challenges of life. The lyrics portrayal of inner fears and the struggle to articulate one's thoughts (*before my tongue has tripped me*) highlight the existential journey of self-discovery and the quest for authenticity amidst *existential angst*. These lines highlight the hesitation and anxiety that come from confronting the uncertainties of human existence. The fear and anxiety are present long before any action is taken, emphasising the internal struggle with the unknown and the ambiguous nature of life decisions.

The lyrics *Must I always be alone* reflect the realisation of one's freedom and the isolation that can accompany it. The question of whether one must always be alone points to the individual's struggle with the burden of making meaningful connections and choices in a world where they are ultimately responsible for creating their own purpose. Similarly, the lyrics convey a sense of *existential dread* and uncertainty and reflect the fear of isolation and the existential questioning of one's place in the world.

Kierkegaard emphasises that faith is a personal and subjective experience that cannot be fully understood or communicated through objective means. He argues that each individual's faith journey is unique and deeply personal, shaped by their subjective experiences and beliefs. The lyrics capture this aspect of faith by portraying the speaker's internal struggle and introspection. The lyrics express a profound longing for connection, evident in the questioning of being alone. This longing reflects the innate human need for companionship and understanding, highlighting the importance of interpersonal relationships in the quest for meaning. The speaker's fear of solitude underscores the significance of these connections in alleviating existential isolation and finding solace amidst inner turmoil.

Kierkegaard posits that *existential dread* stems from the responsibility of shaping one's own life, and this is reflected in the hesitation and anxiety portrayed in the lyrics. The struggle to articulate thoughts highlights the challenge of self-discovery and authenticity amidst uncertainty. Kierkegaard's idea of the *leap-of-faith* suggests that embracing solitude and uncertainty is necessary for living authentically, and the lyrics encapsulate this tension between existential loneliness and the yearning for connection.

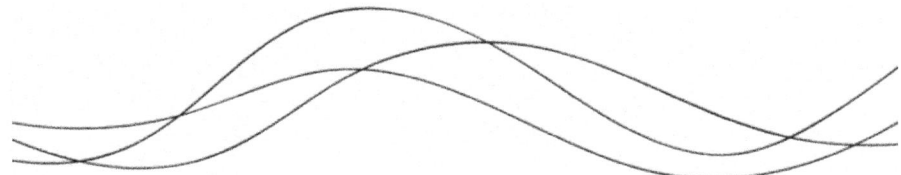

Bonnie Tyler

Total Eclipse of the Heart

Together we can take it to the end of the line
Your love is like a shadow on me all of the time (all of the time)

These lyrics express a sentiment of enduring love and a sense of being constantly accompanied or overshadowed by it. These themes can be linked to the philosophical ideas of Plato, particularly his concept of love as depicted in his dialogue, *Symposium*.

Symposium

Plato's *Symposium* offers a rich exploration of the nature of love, presenting it as a multifaceted concept that encompasses both physical and metaphysical dimensions. In the dialogue, various characters deliver speeches that articulate different aspects of love, reflecting Plato's nuanced understanding of this complex emotion. Firstly, Plato acknowledges the physical dimension of love, often associated with desire and attraction. This aspect of love is evident in speeches such as that of Phaedrus, who describes love as a motivating force that inspires individuals to pursue greatness and achieve noble deeds in the name of their beloved. This physical aspect of love is characterised by its passionate and sensual nature, driving individuals to seek union with their beloved on a psychical level.

However, Plato goes beyond mere physical attraction and delves into the metaphysical dimensions of love. Through speeches like that of Diotima, Plato introduces the concept of *Platonic Love*, which transcends the physical realm and encompasses spiritual and intellectual connections between individuals. According to Diotima, love is a ladder of ascent towards the divine, culminating in the union of souls, where individuals transcend their individual identities and merge into a higher state of being. This union represents the fulfilment of the longing for completeness, as individuals find unity and harmony with their beloved on a spiritual and existential level.

Plato's portrayal of love as both physical and metaphysical highlights its complexity and richness as a philosophical concept. Love, in the Platonic sense, is not merely an emotion or a bodily impulse but a profound yearning for connection, understanding, and transcendence. It encompasses both the earthly desires of the body and the lofty aspirations of the soul, bridging the gap between the material and the spiritual realms. Plato also suggests that romantic love reflects a desire for immortality, as individuals seek to transcend their mortal limitations through their connection with the beloved. The idea of love as a means to achieve lasting significance and transcendence is evident in speeches such as that of Phaedrus, who describes love as a motivating force that inspires individuals to pursue greatness and achieve immortality through their deeds. This desire for immortality underscores the profound significance of romantic love as a means to transcend the ephemeral.

Plato's philosophy introduces the concept of the *Realm of Forms*, which says that the physical world is merely a shadowy reflection of a higher, transcendent realm where ideal and immutable forms exist. This metaphysical framework suggests behind the ever-changing world perceived through the senses lies a realm of perfect and unchanging forms or ideas. These Forms, such as *Justice*, *Beauty*, and *Goodness*, represent the ultimate reality, unchanging and eternal, while the physical world we experience is a mere imitation, constantly changing and imperfect. Love, in Plato's view, transcends the fleeting and superficial experiences of affection or desire that we encounter in the material world, guiding the soul toward a deeper understanding of the ideal. The manifestations of love in the physical world, whether romantic attraction, emotional desire, or fleeting affection, are merely shadows of the ideal *Form of Love* that exists in the Realm of Forms. According to Plato, love in its truest, most profound sense is not confined to the physical or emotional experiences of human beings but is a desire to move closer to the perfect and divine Form of Love itself. Through love, individuals are called to recognise the imperfection of the material world and strive toward the ideal, striving for beauty, goodness, and truth in a way that aligns with the divine essence of the Forms.

The Lyrics

The lyrics hint at the metaphysical dimension of love through the imagery of the beloved's love being like a shadow on the speaker all the time. This metaphor suggests a profound and enduring connection that transcends physical presence, echoing Plato's concept of *platonic love* as a spiritual and intellectual bond between individuals. The idea of love as a constant presence, like a shadow, evokes the notion of love as a timeless and transcendent force that shapes and enriches one's existence. Furthermore, the lyrics hint at a desire for immortality through the enduring nature of the beloved's love, which is likened to a shadow that is always present. This suggests a yearning for a love that transcends the temporal and offers a sense of lasting significance and transcendence, akin to Plato's notion of love as a means to achieve immortality through union with the beloved.

The lyrics expression of being accompanied by *love all of the time* suggests a sense of unity and connection that also transcends physical presence, echoing Plato's vision of love as a transformative force that unites souls. The lyrics suggests a deep and constant presence of the beloved's love, which transcends the fleeting nature of physical desire. This echoes Plato's idea of love as an ascent from the physical realm to a higher form of connection, where individuals move beyond the limitations of the physical world to attain a deeper, more profound understanding of love. Furthermore, the lyrics hint at a journey of self-discovery and transformation through love.

The phrase *Together we can take it to the end of the line* suggests a shared journey towards self-realisation and enlightenment, akin to Plato's notion of love as a transformative force that enables individuals to transcend their earthly limitations and attain a higher state of being. Through their connection with their soulmate, individuals are able to embark on a journey of self-discovery and growth, ultimately finding solace and harmony in the embrace of their other half. This phrase also suggests a physical closeness and shared journey with the beloved, reflecting the passionate and intimate nature of romantic love.

This aspect aligns with the portrayal of love in the *Symposium* as a force that drives individuals to seek union with their beloved on a bodily level, as seen in speeches like that of Phaedrus. It suggests a shared journey, symbolising the pursuit of higher truths and ideals. In the context of Plato's philosophy, this could represent the ascent of the soul towards the Realm of Forms, where eternal, perfect truths exist. The journey is not just physical, but intellectual and spiritual, as love, in this case, serves as the guiding force toward self-realisation and the union with the divine.

The theme of unity in these lyrics suggests a connection that surpasses the limits of time and space, reflecting the Platonic ideal of love as a means of self-discovery and personal growth. The lyrics hint at a longing for immortality through love's lasting impact, mirroring Plato's belief that love offers a path to transcendence. Additionally, the imagery of a shared journey with a soulmate symbolises the pursuit of deeper truths and enlightenment, echoing Plato's idea that love leads individuals beyond the physical world toward ultimate wisdom. The lyrics ultimately present love as both a passionate and spiritual force, capable of guiding individuals toward self-realisation and fulfilment.

Rick Springfield

Jessie's Girl

♪ And I'm lookin' in the mirror all the time
Wonderin' what she don't see in me

These lyrics express a sense of self-reflection, insecurity, and a longing for validation or understanding from another person. These themes resonate with the philosophical ideas of Jean-Paul Sartre, particularly his exploration of the concept of *'the other'*, *'the look'* and the experience of *existential alienation*.

The Look

Sartre placed significant emphasis on the role of *the other* in shaping one's sense of self. His ideas explore how interactions with others fundamentally impact our identity, freedom, and self-perception. Sartre's famous dictum, *"existence precedes essence"* asserts that individuals first exist without any predetermined purpose or essence and must create their own identities through actions and choices. However, this process of self-creation is deeply influenced by the presence of others. The gaze of *the other* forces individuals to confront themselves, often revealing aspects of their identity they might prefer to ignore or deny.

In his work *Being and Nothingness*, Sartre introduced the concept of *the look* (le regard), describing how being seen by another person can make one feel objectified and aware of oneself as an object in the world. This experience of being gazed at by *the other* can lead to feelings of shame or pride, as individuals become acutely aware of how they are perceived. The gaze of *the other* transforms a person from a free, subjective being into an object in someone else's world, thus shaping their sense of self. Sartre's idea of *the look* is pivotal in understanding existential alienation. When we become aware that someone else is looking at us, we begin to see ourselves through their eyes. This external perspective can make us feel objectified, as if we are being reduced to an object in their world. Instead of being a free, autonomous subject, we feel like we are a thing, subject to the other person's interpretation and judgment.

According to Sartre, self-consciousness arises through the recognition of being seen by others. The awareness of being observed and judged by others compels individuals to see themselves from an external perspective. This duality, seeing oneself as both subject and object, creates a complex and often conflicted sense of self, as people strive to reconcile their internal self-perception with how they are perceived by others. In our everyday experience, we perceive ourselves as subjects, actively engaging with the world. However, under the gaze of another, we become conscious of ourselves as objects. This shift from being the one who looks to being the one who is looked at can create a profound sense of alienation. We lose our sense of being a subject with our own intrinsic identity and feel defined by how others see us.

Sartre emphasises that while the presence of *the other* can be constraining, it also underscores the inherent freedom and responsibility of the individual. Even as individuals are influenced by the perceptions and judgments of others, they remain free to choose how they respond and define themselves. This interaction with *the other* highlights the tension between one's autonomy and the social dimensions of existence. This feeling of being objectified by the gaze of another leads to existential alienation. It's a sense of estrangement from our own identity and freedom. We become aware of the disparity between our self-perception and the way others perceive us. This alienation can cause discomfort, anxiety, or even shame, as we struggle with the realisation that our self-concept is partly constructed by how others see us.

Sartre argues that this dynamic is inescapable in human relationships. Every interaction with another person involves this dual perspective, our own subjective view of ourselves and the objective view imposed by others. This duality complicates our efforts to define our own identity independently.

The Look in these Lyrics

The lyrics mention of *lookin' in the mirror all the time* suggesting a preoccupation with self-image and identity, while the wondering about what another person *don't see in me* reflects a desire for recognition and understanding from *the other*. Sartre's concept of *the look* highlights how the perception of others shapes our own self-awareness. In the lyrics, the speaker's constant self-reflection in the mirror and their wonder about what *she* doesn't see in them indicate a preoccupation with how they are perceived by beloved *other*. Sartre discusses how being aware of another's *look* can make one feel objectified, leading to an internal conflict between one's own view of themselves and the perception they imagine others have. The speaker's introspection is a response to this objectification, reflecting Sartre's notion of the struggle to assert one's own identity in the face of external judgments. The speaker's repeated self-examination in the mirror indicates a loss of subjectivity. They are viewing themselves from an external perspective, trying to understand how they appear in the eyes of their beloved

This reflects Sartre's idea that our sense of self is deeply influenced by the way others see us. The speaker's identity and self-worth are being questioned and defined through the eyes of the beloved, illustrating the impact of *the other's* gaze. The lyrics portrayal of looking in the mirror and wondering about the perception of *the other* alludes to this sense of being defined or judged by external standards, leading to feelings of insecurity and inadequacy. The act of looking in the mirror and questioning what the beloved doesn't see in them signifies a conflict between the speaker's self-perception and how they believe they are perceived by *the other*. The speaker feels reduced to an object of her judgment, wondering why they doesn't see certain qualities in them. This encapsulates Sartre's notion of how another's *look* can make us feel like an object rather than a free subject.

The speaker in the lyrics is preoccupied with how they are perceived by the beloved, reflecting Sartre's idea of external judgments shaping self-perception. The speaker's constant mirror-gazing and questioning (*Wonderin' what she don't see in me*) illustrates the impact of the beloved's gaze on their self-identity. This continuous self-examination and questioning reflects existential angst, a core theme in Sartre's philosophy. This angst arises from the realisation of one's freedom and the burden of defining oneself in a world where others' perceptions constantly intrude. The lyrics capture this angst as the speaker grapples with their own identity and worth, heavily influenced by the beloved's gaze.

The existential alienation Sartre describes is vividly reflected in the speaker's feelings of inadequacy and doubt as the speaker grapples with their own sense of self in relation to the perceptions of others. The lyrics reveal a conflict between the speaker's self-view and the beloved's view. The self-questioning highlights the speaker's attempt to reconcile their own identity with the perceived judgment of their beloved. This tension reflects Sartre's idea that human relationships involve a dual perspective, how we see ourselves versus how we believe others see us, leading to alienation when these views conflict. The lyrics convey a sense of anguish and self-doubt, reflecting Sartre's notion of the existential burden of responsibility. The speaker's continuous questioning (*Wonderin' what she don't see in me*), captures the anxiety that comes with the freedom to define oneself and the responsibility to live authentically. The anguish stems from the realisation that their self-worth cannot be passively received from the beloved but must be actively created and owned.

The lyrics capture the tension between subjective identity and external validation, illustrating how human relationships often involve a struggle between authenticity and the influence of others' judgments. The existential anxiety expressed in the lyrics stems from the realisation that self-worth cannot be granted by another but must be defined independently, highlighting Sartre's notion of personal responsibility and the challenge of living authentically in a world shaped by external perceptions.

Culture Club

Karma Chameleon

 I'm a man without conviction
I'm a man who doesn't know
How to sell a contradiction

These lyrics can be understood within the philosophical ideas of Friedrich Nietzsche, particularly his concepts of perspectivism and the nature of truth.

Perspectivism:
Nietzsche's rejection of the traditional notion of an objective, singular truth is one of the cornerstones of his philosophy, and it stands in sharp contrast to the classical, Enlightenment-era ideas that truth is something universal, immutable, and independent of human perception. For Nietzsche, the concept of truth is fluid and relative, it is not something that exists *'out there'* as an objective reality to be discovered, but rather something that is created, shaped by an individual's perspective, values, and lived experiences.

Nietzsche believed that traditional truths, especially those propagated by religious institutions and social norms, were often imposed by those in power to control the masses. For instance, the concepts of morality and objective truth promoted by religious institutions were, in his view, tools used to maintain authority and suppress individual freedom. These truths were not discovered by free individuals through their own experience and self-exploration, but were handed down from external authorities that shaped the way people saw the world. Rather than assuming truth is fixed, Nietzsche proposed that truth is inherently subjective, shaped by the individual's perspective. His concept of perspectivism holds that there is no one *true* way to see the world, instead, there are many truths, each shaped by the unique perspective, context, and experiences of the person perceiving it. This is not relativism in the sense that any belief is as valid as any other, rather, Nietzsche suggested that truths are always intertwined with power relations and are inseparable from the personal forces that create them.

For Nietzsche, an individual is not a passive receiver of truth, but an active creator of it. The truths we live by are a reflection of our *will-to-power*, our capacity to assert and shape reality through our own perspectives. For instance, two people might observe the same event but interpret it in vastly different ways based on their past experiences, desires, and values. One person might see a public protest as a fight for justice, while another might view it as a dangerous rebellion. Nietzsche would argue that both perspectives are valid, not because one is objectively true, but because each is a product of the individual's unique perspective and life experience. In this way, Nietzsche rejects the idea of a single, objective truth, seeing instead a multiplicity of truths that reflect the diversity of human experience.

One of the most radical aspects of Nietzsche's philosophy is his insistence that contradictions are not problems to be solved but inseparable aspects of life. The tension between conflicting truths or perspectives is part of the process of self-creation and self-overcoming. Human beings live in a world full of contradictions, both within themselves and in the world around them. These contradictions may be internal, as when a person holds two opposing desires or values, or external, as when different groups or individuals clash over competing truths or perspectives. For Nietzsche, the resolution of contradiction does not mean eliminating it or forcing it into a neat, unified system. Instead, contradiction is a stimulus for growth. The individual who embraces contradiction is someone who is engaged in the process of self-creation. By accepting the contradictions within themselves, a person can transcend their former limitations and become something new.

Nietzsche's concept of the *Übermensch* (or *"Overman"*) encapsulates this idea. The *Übermensch* is the individual who has fully embraced their own will to power, who has transcended conventional morality and external truths to create their own values. This process involves accepting the contradictions within oneself, integrating them into a new, dynamic whole, and creating a life that is authentic and self-determined. The struggle with contradiction, far from being an obstacle, becomes an opportunity for growth and empowerment.

This is particularly relevant in the modern world, where individuals are often encouraged to choose one identity, one truth, or one way of being. For Nietzsche, the true challenge is learning to live with ambiguity and tension, and recognising that life itself is a process of becoming, not a static state of being. The inability to reconcile contradictions could also reflect a fear of chaos, a fear that without a singular, unified truth, life will be meaningless or fragmented. Nietzsche, however, suggests that the opposite is true, that embracing contradictions opens the possibility for a much richer, more creative existence, where individuals can define their own truths and actively engage with the world in a way that reflects their personal power and will to create meaning.

Perspectivism in these Lyrics
The phrase *without conviction* suggests more than simple uncertainty, it implies an absence of personal autonomy in defining values and beliefs. Nietzsche argues that individuals who

lack conviction have not engaged in the difficult process of self-overcoming, instead allowing societal, religious, or external influences to dictate their worldview. This aligns with his concept of slave morality, where values are passively inherited rather than actively created. The person without conviction exists in a state of dependence, unable to establish their own guiding principles. In contrast, the *Übermensch* is the individual who actively shapes their own values, forging meaning through personal strength and self-determination. The man *without conviction* is therefore caught in a liminal space, unable to transcend external influences and move toward true self-actualization.

The lyric *I'm a man who doesn't know how to sell a contradiction* further deepens this existential struggle, reflecting a fundamental difficulty in reconciling competing truths or perspectives. Nietzsche's concept of *perspectivism* suggests that truth is not singular or objective but rather shaped by different viewpoints and interpretations. To "*sell a contradiction*" can mean to navigate, embrace, or communicate this multiplicity of truths, something the speaker appears unable to do. This hesitation could indicate a resistance to confronting the inherent contradictions of existence or a failure to integrate opposing beliefs into a coherent sense of self. The *Übermensch*, in contrast, thrives in this complexity, forging meaning from it rather than being paralysed by it.

Nietzsche also emphasizes that human understanding is always limited by perspective, meaning contradictions are an unavoidable part of reality. The speaker's struggle suggests an individual caught between awareness of this complexity and an inability to fully engage with it. The refusal or inability to *sell* contradiction might represent a deeper existential paralysis. An unwillingness to embrace ambiguity, change, or the responsibility of creating meaning. Instead of actively shaping their worldview, they remain trapped in self-doubt, unable to progress toward the self-mastery that Nietzsche sees as essential to true freedom.

Exploring themes of self-doubt, identity, and the struggle to define one's own beliefs, these lyrics reflect a sense of uncertainty and passivity, where the speaker seems unable to commit to a clear sense of self or purpose. This aligns with broader philosophical ideas about the tension between external influences and personal authenticity. The mention of contradictions suggests an inner conflict, highlighting the difficulty of navigating complex or opposing truths. Overall, the lyrics convey a struggle with self-definition and the challenge of finding personal conviction in a world of shifting perspectives.

Whitney Houston

I Want to Dance with Somebody

Clock strikes upon the hour
And the sun begins to fade
Still enough time to figure out
How to chase my blues away

These lyrics evoke themes of time, change, and self-reflection, which are evident in the philosophical ideas of Martin Heidegger, particularly his exploration of existential temporality and the concept of being-towards-death.

Temporal Existence

Heidegger argues that human existence (which he terms *Dasein*, meaning *'being there'*) is always situated in time. Unlike traditional views that treat time as an external, abstract concept (*i.e. a sequence of moments*), Heidegger suggests that time is central to the way we experience and understand ourselves. In his view, we are not passive subjects who simply experience time, instead we are in time, and it shapes who we are and how we live.

Temporal existence, for Heidegger, is not linear. It's not just about past, present, and future as discrete, objective categories. *Dasein* exists as a constant movement through time, always oriented by the past (*which influences the present*), but more importantly, it is always projecting itself toward the future, toward what it might become. Heidegger stresses that human beings are fundamentally future-oriented because they always make plans, set goals, and project themselves into the future. However, this future projection is not merely about achieving goals in a conventional sense. It is about confronting the open possibilities of what one can become.

Heidegger asserts that *Dasein* is always aware, even if unconsciously, of its own finitude. Human beings are unique in that they know they will die. This awareness of mortality shapes our existence in profound ways. According to Heidegger, we are *being-towards-death* because the possibility of death is always present in our lives, even though we may not always be actively conscious of it. Rather than seeing death as an abstract concept or something that happens at the end of life, Heidegger argues that it is an essential part of human existence and must be fully recognised. Death is not a distant event to be feared in the future, but an ever-present possibility that shapes the choices we make and the way we experience life. The more we acknowledge our finitude, the more authentically we can live.

For Heidegger, living authentically means accepting the inevitability of death and facing it with openness. This involves an honest confrontation with our own limitations and the choices we make in light of those limitations. *Authenticity* is about living in a way that is true to oneself, unencumbered by the distractions and conventionalities imposed by society. In contrast, inauthenticity is the way many people live in denial of death, living instead in a way that conforms to social norms or clings to distractions, avoiding deeper reflection on life's finite nature.

A key component of Heidegger's existential philosophy is the notion of *care* (*Sorge*), which refers to the fundamental way in which we are engaged with the world. Care expresses the idea that human existence is not passive but active, we are always engaged in our world, concerned with our surroundings, our projects, and our future. This concern for our existence shapes the way we experience and interpret the world. Care is not just a feeling of worry or anxiety, it is an existential state that reflects our ongoing need to make sense of ourselves and our place in the world. It is through care that we project ourselves into the future and make decisions that shape our lives. However, care also includes anxiety, which emerges when we confront the vastness of our freedom and the uncertainty of our existence. Anxiety is the experience of realising that we are ultimately alone in our freedom, responsible for our own choices, and that our time is finite.

Temporal Existence in these Lyrics

Clock strikes upon the hour / And the sun begins to fade highlight, in Heideggerian terms, the awareness of time's passage. That it is not just as a measurement of moments but a lived experience that we are inseparable from. The clock striking and the sun fading symbolise the inescapable march of time and the inevitability of change. This reflects Heidegger's concept of *temporal existence*, we are not static beings, but always moving through time, never detached from it.

The clock and sun both signal the movement of time, not in the abstract sense but as something that directly impacts the person experiencing it. The fading sun can evoke a sense of life's impermanence, a constant reminder that the present moment is always slipping away. The awareness of the inevitable end i.e. our mortality. The setting sun symbolises the approach of death, which, for Heidegger, is always present in our consciousness, shaping how we live.

In the lyrics *Still enough time to figure out / How to chase my blues away* the speaker expresses a desire to find resolution or solace within the confines of time. Heidegger's notion of *being-towards-death* emphasises that awareness of our finite existence propels us to seek meaning, purpose, and authenticity. '*Still enough time*' reveal a tension between the limited nature of time and the possibility of action, it also suggests an active attempt to find a way out of emotional distress, a desire to live more authentically despite the transient nature of time. There's a subtle sense of urgency, pushing the speaker toward action in the face of life's impermanence. If the speaker simply accepted the fading of the sun without seeking resolution, it might be seen as an inauthentic response, one that accepts despair or resignation without fighting for meaning.

Reflecting the concept of care (*Sorge*), 'how to chase my blues away' notes the emotional and existential concern for one's state of being. The speaker's attempt to overcome sadness or confusion can be seen as a manifestation of care, the fundamental human engagement with the world. In Heidegger's terms, the struggle to find solace amidst time's passage is part of the existential care we experience as we project ourselves into the future and try to make meaning of our existence.

The act of trying to resolve emotional distress is a way of engaging with the world and confronting existential challenges. Heidegger argues that facing our anxiety about time and death can lead to more authentic living. In this sense, the lyrics reflect the internal struggle to come to terms with existential angst, an effort to confront and resolve one's emotions, which is part of living authentically. There's a subtle tension between recognising that time is passing and the desire to do something about it, to escape sadness or find meaning before it's too late. Heidegger would interpret this as a recognition of the urgency of making one's existence meaningful in the face of death.

Survivor

Eye of the Tiger

So many times, it happens too fast
You trade your passion for glory
Don't lose your grip on the dreams of the past
You must fight just to keep them alive

These lyrics reflects themes of individuality, societal expectations, and the repression of certain aspects of the self, which are directly mirrored in the psychological ideas of Carl Jung, particularly his concept of the *persona*, the *shadow* and the *Diminution of Personality*.

Diminution of Personality

Jung's philosophy, speaks to the conflict between individuality and conformity. One key concept he explores is the idea that modern society places immense pressure on individuals to conform to externally defined standards of success, such as wealth, fame, power, or social approval. As a result, individuals often trade their personal desires, passions, and creative inclinations for these societal rewards. Jung argued that the pursuit of these external achievements often leads to a *diminution of personality*. This means that in order to succeed in the social world, a person may suppress or neglect certain aspects of their true self. These aspects might include personal dreams, deeper emotional experiences, or even unconscious parts of their psyche that are not valued by society. As people chase external success, they may forget or abandon these more personal, soulful parts of who they are.

Jung believed that a person's *personality* is not just their surface identity, but a complex, multidimensional being with unconscious elements that often remain unexplored. He warned that an overemphasis on external achievement leads to a loss of the full richness of the self. When we focus only on meeting societal expectations, we can miss the opportunity for a more profound, integrated sense of who we truly are. Jung used powerful metaphors to describe the parts of ourselves that get left behind. He referred to these neglected aspects of our psyche as being placed in the *lumber-room among dusty memories* to represent the thought that many vital components of who we are, our deepest desires, childhood dreams, or even unexpressed emotions, are cast aside and forgotten in the rush toward success. The *lumber-room* is a place where these parts are stored away, almost as if they are of no real use anymore.

Sometimes, Jung said, these abandoned parts of ourselves do not simply vanish but *remain like glowing coals under grey ashes*. Even though they may be hidden or neglected, they still hold energy and vitality. The *coals* symbolise forgotten or suppressed aspects of the self that retain power, though obscured by the weight of time and societal pressures. If left unattended, these coals can turn into emotional or psychological problems, creating tension or even crisis when they inevitably resurface.

Jung's deeper message is that true wholeness and authenticity come not from conforming to external expectations, but from integrating these lost or hidden aspects of the self. This integration process, known as *individuation*, involves reconnecting with the parts of oneself that have been abandoned or ignored. It requires a conscious effort to reclaim the neglected aspects of one's personality, desires, and dreams, those coals that have been smothered by the ashes of societal pressures. Individuation is not about rejecting societal success or external rewards, but rather about finding a balance where a person can achieve these external goals without sacrificing the more personal, meaningful parts of their self. Jung believed that individuals must constantly engage in this process of self-reflection and integration to maintain their psychological and emotional health, and to live authentically.

Diminution of Personality in these Lyrics

So many times, it happens too fast, speaks to the rapid pace at which individuals often make choices driven by external pressures. Jung would argue that people can become so absorbed in the demands of the external world (*like career, success, and social status*) that they don't realise how quickly they are sacrificing parts of their authentic selves. Just as Jung suggests, these neglected parts end up "among dusty memories," buried in the unconscious, and the individual becomes less whole over time. The *too fast* aspect highlights how these shifts can occur without full awareness, leading to a gradual erosion of personality. Jung's concept of the *diminution of personality* describes how, in our rush to meet societal expectations, we lose touch with the deeper, more meaningful parts of ourselves.

You trade your passion for glory explicitly mirrors one of Jung's key critiques, that people often *trade* their deeper, authentic desires (*their passions*) for external rewards (*glory*). Glory, in this case, can be understood as societal validation, wealth, fame, recognition, or status. Things that are externally defined and often come with the cost of personal sacrifice. Jung believed that chasing external success often led to the abandonment of one's true self. This *trade* symbolises the moment when a person sacrifices their passions, things that give life meaning and depth, in exchange for something that may seem valuable on the surface but is ultimately hollow if it comes at the cost of personal authenticity. The *glory* may offer temporary satisfaction, but it can leave the individual feeling disconnected from their true desires, just as Jung's concept of the lost, unintegrated parts of the self suggests.

Don't lose your grip on the dreams of the past encourages holding onto *the dreams of the past*, which can be interpreted as a call to preserve the deep, personal aspects of the self that were once vivid but may now be forgotten or suppressed in the pursuit of societal achievements. Jung's metaphor of the *lumber-room among dusty memories* fits perfectly here. The "*dreams of the past* represent those parts of the self that may have been pushed aside in favour of more practical or socially valued pursuits. The line emphasises the importance of holding onto these dreams, not letting them fade or be buried under the weight of external demands.

Jung believed that these past dreams are not merely youthful fantasies or distractions, but core components of a person's identity that can provide guidance and meaning. Losing grip on them can result in losing touch with one's true self. This line, then, is a reminder to protect and nurture these inner desires, as they are vital for psychological wholeness. *You must fight just to keep them alive* brings the message to a crucial point, it takes effort, struggle, and awareness to preserve the core of who you are in a world that often pushes you to conform. The word fight here suggests that keeping the deeper parts of yourself alive requires vigilance and active engagement. It means resisting the temptation to let those parts of your personality fade away in favour of external rewards.

It's not always easy to resist societal pressure, and it takes conscious effort to reconnect with those buried, authentic parts of the self. Individuation is not a passive journey, it requires conscious effort to resist external pressures and reconnect with the buried, authentic parts of oneself. Without this struggle, one risks falling into what Jung called psychic stagnation, where the unintegrated aspects of the self-remain in the shadows, leading to a life of fragmentation and unfulfilled potential. Jung likened the unconscious aspects of the self to *glowing embers buried beneath the ashes*, waiting to be reignited. The fight to keep them alive is the fight to reconnect with one's deepest drives, passions, and unique essence before they are entirely smothered by societal expectations.

To Jung, true psychological health is found in this ongoing engagement with both the conscious and unconscious self, ensuring that the embers of one's individuality continue to glow rather than fading into cold ash.

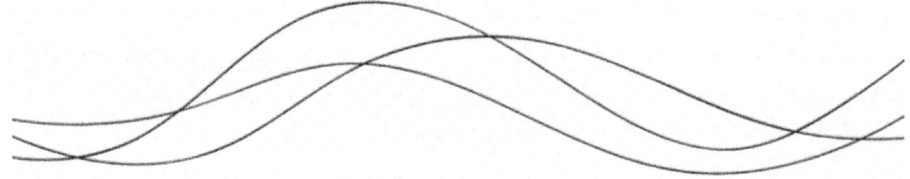

Van Halen

Jump

♪ And I know, baby, just how you feel
You got to roll with the punches to get to what's real

These lyrics resonate with the philosophy of Albert Camus, a philosopher often associated with existentialism and absurdism, in particular his philosophy of embracing life's absurdities.

The Philosophy of Absurdity

Albert Camus explored the concept of the absurd in works like *The Myth of Sisyphus*. His philosophy centres on the conflict between two fundamental truths; 1) Human Beings Seek Meaning: Humans have an innate desire to find meaning, purpose, and order in life. We ask profound questions about existence, morality, and our place in the universe. And 2) The Universe Is Indifferent: The universe offers no inherent meaning or answers to our questions. It is vast, indifferent, and chaotic. The more we search for definitive meaning, the more we encounter the silence of the universe.

This conflict, the human yearning for meaning versus the universe's indifference, is what Camus calls the absurd. Camus argues that when confronted with the absurd, humans have three possible responses:

1. Suicide: *This is the choice to escape the absurd by ceasing to exist. Camus rejects this as a solution because it avoids confronting life's challenges and the opportunity to experience life itself.*

2. **Religious or Philosophical Leap:** *Some people try to resolve the absurd by leaping to faith or believing in an external source of meaning (e.g., God or destiny). Camus rejects this as well, calling it an act of intellectual dishonesty. To him, such leaps involve surrendering reason and accepting a fabricated purpose.*

3. **Acceptance (Revolt):** *Camus champions this response. Acceptance involves recognising the absurd, embracing it without trying to resolve it, and choosing to live fully and freely despite it. This defiance is a form of rebellion, a way to assert human dignity and freedom in a meaningless world.*

Camus sees rebellion as the ultimate response to the absurd. To rebel is not to fight against the absurd in hopes of defeating it (*since it cannot be defeated*), but rather to live authentically and embrace life as it is. This involves embracing the here and now instead of yearning for some higher purpose. Finding joy, beauty, and fulfilment in the small, tangible aspects of life. relationships, art, work, and nature. Recognising that without inherent meaning, we are free to create our own purpose and live by our own values.

Camus uses the Greek myth of Sisyphus as a metaphor for human existence. Sisyphus is condemned to roll a boulder up a hill for eternity, only for it to roll back down every time. Camus reimagines Sisyphus as a symbol of rebellion. Despite the futility of his task, Sisyphus continues to push the boulder, finding freedom in his acceptance of his fate. In this, Camus declares: 'One must imagine Sisyphus happy'. This illustrates how embracing life's absurdities allows us to live with passion and freedom, even in the face of inevitable struggles.

The Philosophy of Absurdity in these Lyrics

And I know, baby, just how you feel expresses empathy and a shared understanding of the challenges of life. In Camus' philosophy, the human condition is universal, everyone grapples with the tension between seeking meaning and confronting a universe that offers none, the sense that life lacks ultimate purpose and yet we yearn for it. The lyric implies a connection between two individuals who both experience this tension, mirroring Camus' acknowledgment that no one is immune to the absurd. It's a moment of solidarity in facing life's inherent difficulties, a recognition that *'I get it—this is hard for all of us'*.

You got to roll with the punches perfectly captures Camus' prescription for dealing with the absurd, acceptance and rebellion. Camus likens human existence to Sisyphus' eternal task of rolling a boulder up a hill, only for it to roll back down each time. The *punches* in the lyric represent life's unpredictability, hardships, and the lack of any ultimate fairness or resolution. Camus asserts that these struggles are intrinsic to existence; they are part of the absurd condition. Life doesn't *'make sense'* or follow our expectations, just as punches don't follow a clear pattern. They come unexpectedly, and their very randomness underscores the absurd. Rather than resisting the absurd or succumbing to despair, Camus advocates for acceptance. *Rolling with the punches* is a metaphor for adapting to life's chaos and refusing to let it break you. This attitude reflects Camus' revolt, not an act of fighting against the absurd (*which is futile*) but an act of embracing it and continuing to live fully despite it.

To get to what's real ties directly to Camus' vision of authentic living and the pursuit of meaning within the absurd. For Camus, *what's real* is not some grand, external truth or divine purpose, but the experiences and moments we create for ourselves. Camus emphasises that meaning is not waiting to be discovered in some ultimate goal or higher power. Instead *what's real* exists in the present, the tangible, immediate experiences of life. By enduring struggles and embracing life as it is, we uncover genuine moments of beauty, joy, and connection. For instance, Sisyphus' task is futile, but in his conscious rebellion, his decision to keep pushing the boulder, he finds freedom and purpose. Similarly *getting to what's real* implies finding meaning not by escaping hardship but by engaging with life authentically, even in its difficulties.

The lyric implies that life's punches (*challenges*) are not obstacles to reality but the very means of accessing it. This reflects Camus' belief that accepting the absurd is the first step toward a fulfilling existence. Without illusions or denial, we can confront life honestly and find profound value in our experiences.
Like Camus, the lyrics acknowledge the inherent struggles of life, symbolised by *punches*. There's an understanding that life can feel harsh, confusing, and devoid of clear meaning. The idea of *rolling* suggests adaptability and acceptance, essential aspects of Camus' revolt. Instead of resisting the chaos of existence or seeking escape, the lyric embraces life's difficulties as part of the journey. The lyrics suggests that authenticity and truth come not from avoiding life's challenges but from engaging with them head-on. For Camus, the act of living itself, immersing oneself in the present and embracing freedom, is what makes life meaningful. This is symbolised by *what's real*, not an external truth, but the honest, raw experiences we cultivate through perseverance.

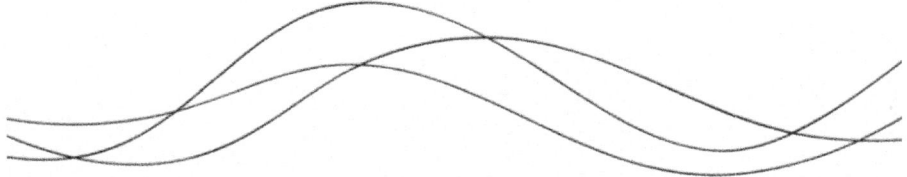

Guns N' Rose

Sweet Child o' Mine

Was a time when I wasn't sure
But you set my mind at ease
There is no doubt you're in my heart now

These lyrics resonate with themes of trust, reassurance, and emotional connection, which are part of the philosophical concept of intersubjectivity, particularly as discussed by Edmund Husserl.

Intersubjectivity

Intersubjectivity refers to the shared experience of consciousness between individuals. Husserl developed this concept to address the fundamental question, *How do we, as conscious beings, recognise and relate to others as subjects like ourselves, and how does this relationship shape our experience of reality?* Husserl uses intersubjectivity to describe how individual subjectivities interact and co-create a shared understanding of the world. It is not merely a form of social interaction but a deeper structure underpinning human experience and the constitution of reality.

While subjectivity focuses on the individual's inner consciousness, intersubjectivity emphasises the relational aspect, how individuals encounter and understand others as conscious beings. For Husserl, the world we experience is not a private construct but a shared one, made meaningful through our interrelations with others. Empathy is the primary mechanism through which intersubjectivity occurs. It allows us to recognise others as conscious subjects with their own experiences and perspectives.

Empathy involves perceiving another person's physical presence (*e.g., body language, facial expressions*) and intuitively grasping that they have a subjective experience similar to ours.

For example, when we see someone smiling, we recognise this as an expression of joy, not merely as a physical movement. This recognition bridges the gap between *my* consciousness and *yours*. Empathy does not mean merging with the other's experience. Instead, it preserves the distinction between self and other while fostering mutual understanding. When we interact with others, their perceptions often align with ours. This mutual confirmation gives us confidence that the world exists beyond our subjective experience. Another example, if I see a tree and others also see and describe the tree similarly, the tree's existence and properties are confirmed intersubjectively. Beyond the physical world, intersubjectivity also shapes cultural and social meanings. Traditions, norms, and shared practices are created and sustained through collective agreement over time.

Husserl identifies several levels at which intersubjectivity operates:
1. **Primal Intersubjectivity:** This is the immediate and intuitive recognition of the other as a subject. It occurs in face-to-face interactions and is the foundation of interpersonal relationships.
2. **Generative Intersubjectivity**: This involves the intersubjective formation of cultural and historical meaning across generations. It explains how traditions and collective knowledge are passed down, enriching the shared world.
3. **Transcendental Intersubjectivity**: A deeper unity of all conscious beings. This *we* is not a specific group or community but the collective foundation of all human experience. The transcendental *we* ensures that the world is

not an isolated construct of any single consciousness but a shared, universal reality co-constituted by all subjects
4. **Temporal Dimensions of Intersubjectivity:** Intersubjectivity is not static, it unfolds over time:
5. **Shared Temporality**: Human beings share a common experience of time. Events, relationships, and traditions link the past, present, and future in a communal narrative.

Intersubjectivity demonstrates that we are not alone in the world; others exist as subjects, not mere objects. Intersubjectivity requires acknowledging others as full subjects with their own dignity and perspectives. This recognition forms the basis of empathy, respect, and moral responsibility.

Husserl's concept of the *lifeworld* (*Lebenswelt*) expands intersubjectivity by grounding human experience in a shared, pre-reflective reality shaped by culture, history, and social interactions. It is the foundation upon which meaning is built, providing the context that makes intersubjective experiences possible. Rather than being a fixed or objective world, the lifeworld is dynamic, evolving through collective participation and generational continuity. Through it, individuals do not just perceive reality but actively co-construct it, reinforcing the idea that our understanding of the world is never purely individual but always shaped by the consciousness of others.

Intersubjectivity in these Lyrics
In the lyrics, the speaker begins with uncertainty (*Was a time when I wasn't sure*). This reflects a state of existential or emotional doubt, which can be likened to a form of isolated subjectivity. Husserl describes how individual consciousness can experience doubt or fragmentation when it lacks a connection to others. The subsequent resolution of this doubt (*But you set my*

mind at ease) highlights the transformative power of intersubjective relationships. In Husserl's framework, the presence of another conscious being, recognised and empathised with, brings reassurance and clarity. The speaker's doubt is resolved not in isolation but through interaction with the *you*, whose actions or understanding stabilise the speaker's world.

In the lyrics, the *you* represents a relational presence that is fully recognised and trusted, creating a bond that transcends mere individual experience. Husserl emphasises empathy as the mechanism through which we recognise others as conscious beings with their own perspectives allows for the sharing of experiences and feelings. The line *There is no doubt you're in my heart now* suggests a deep empathetic connection. For Husserl, such a connection is the foundation of intersubjectivity, where the other is not merely an object in the world but a co-participant in the constitution of shared meaning.

Husserl's philosophy posits that meaning is co-created through intersubjective relationships. The *you* in the lyrics has an active role in shaping the speaker's emotional reality, leading to a new, enriched understanding of their world. The resolution of doubt and the embrace of relational closeness (*you're in my heart now*) illustrate the shift from solitary meaning-making to shared understanding. This process reflects how intersubjectivity allows individuals to transcend their own isolated experiences and participate in a communal horizon of meaning. The speaker's emotional state is no longer self-contained but intertwined with the presence and influence of the other.

Husserl links intersubjectivity to a shared sense of time, where the past, present, and future are experienced in connection with others. The speaker's reference to a prior time of uncertainty and a present state of assurance illustrates how relationships anchor us temporally. The *you* has not only provided reassurance in the present but has likely transformed how the speaker interprets their past and anticipates their future. The shift from doubt to clarity is not just an emotional journey but also a temporal one, highlighting how intersubjectivity enriches the continuity of individual experience.

In Husserl's phenomenology, the lifeworld (*Lebenswelt*) is the shared ground of meaning that arises from intersubjective interactions. The *you* in the lyrics becomes a part of the speaker's *lifeworld*, symbolised by the phrase *you're in my heart now*. This suggests that the relationship has become a foundational element of the speaker's lived reality, shaping their understanding of themselves and the world around them.

While initially the speaker experiences emotional fragmentation, this is transformed through connection with another person. Husserl argues that empathy and recognition of others consciousness are key to resolving such doubts. Meaning, according to Husserl, is co-created through relationships, where individuals transcend isolated experiences to form a shared understanding. This connection also anchors the individual in time, influencing their perception of the past, present, and future. Ultimately, the relationship becomes integral to the speaker's sense of self and world, forming a shared *lifeworld*.

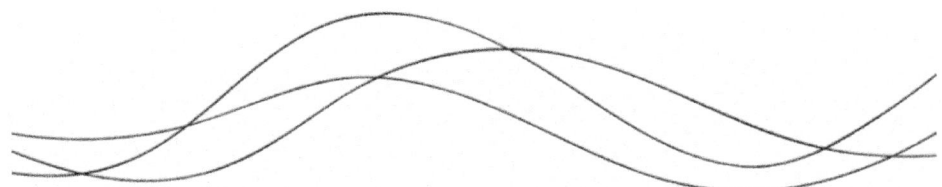

CLOSING THOUGHTS

As we reach the final chords of *Harmonies of Thought*, we find ourselves at the culmination of a journey through the rich interplay of music and philosophy. Throughout this collection, we have explored the lyrical landscapes of human experience, guided by the profound insights of philosophical inquiry.

In these pages, we have encountered the universal themes that unite us all, love and loss, hope and despair, longing and fulfilment. Through the melodies of music and the reflections of philosophy, we have looked into the depths of human emotion and the complexities of existence, discovering anew the timeless truths that resonate across cultures and centuries.

As we say farewell to these pages, we carry with us the echoes of wisdom that have illuminated our path. For *Harmonies of Thought* is not merely a collection of lyrics and philosophers but a testament to the enduring power of human creativity and insight.

In the closing notes of this symphony, let us remember that the pursuit of understanding is an ongoing journey, an ever-unfolding melody that invites us to listen deeply and reflect thoughtfully. As we continue to navigate the currents of life, may we find solace and inspiration in the harmonies of music and the wisdom of philosophy, guiding us toward greater clarity, compassion, and connection.

And so, as we turn the final page let us carry forward the melodies and musings that have touched our hearts and stirred our souls. For in the grand symphony of existence, we are all but players, each contributing our own unique notes to the eternal chorus of humanity.

As the music fades into silence, may we remember that the true beauty lies not in the individual notes but in the harmonies that unite us all.

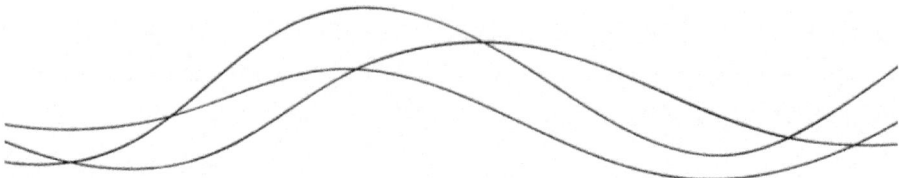

Printed in Great Britain
by Amazon